CAN I GO
HOME WITH YOU?

Written By Alice Hanh
Illustrated by Irene Lee

Dedication:

To James and Bear

To Irene and Remy

To all the donors who made this book possible

To all the special dogs in this book

And to all the past, present, and future rescue dogs and owners

10% of book profit will be donated to Jindo Love Rescue. Learn more at www.jindoloverescue.org.

Bear was convinced he would never get adopted and end up in the Room of No Return. There, he would disappear forever without ever being loved. He had only one day to find his forever home, and luck had not been on his side so far. Bear knew that he was not special like the others were at the shelter.

In the kennel next to him was Annie with her amazing singing voice. And the next kennel over was Nala, a terrific and graceful dancer.

But Bear had never taken voice lessons before and had two clumsy left paws.

There was also Taj, who was really, really

BIG and handsome.

And Dolly, who was really, really
tiny **and adorable.**

But Bear was just medium-sized
and had a funny, toothy smile.

There were others who were from all around the world.

T'va was from Mexico. Smudge was from Iran. Duke was from Bermuda, while Oliver Drew was from South Korea.

Bear didn't have a passport, and he was sure
that plane rides would make him gassy.

Some of the dogs at the shelter were trained to help
and comfort people.

Nona was a PTSD service dog. Lucy and Moxie were therapy dogs.

Bear's best skills were snoring loudly, chasing his tail, and tearing
up his toys (except for his trusty sidekick, Snoth the Sloth).

Some dogs at the shelter had very
sad and scary stories :-(

Bentley had been tied
to a tree.

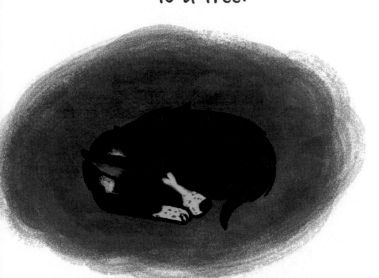

Django was left to sleep in a
dark room alone.

Theo was returned to the
shelter many times.

Bear was not as brave as his friends
were, and he admired their courage.

There were some who had come to the shelter with upsetting injuries. Gypsy had only three legs, and Taj had a twisted paw.

Bear wished his special needs friends would be the first to find their forever homes.

Across from Bear's kennel were Amos, the adventure seeker, and Gracie, the most thoughtful soul.

Then there was Miles, who had a standout chest patch and a dapper grin, and Luna, who had unique and beautiful eyes.

Abby and Otter came in a lovely pair. There was no separating them!

Each dog was so special in their own ways. But Bear was just a black, unmemorable dog.

All day long, people bustled in and out of the shelter. As curious visitors knelt down in front of the kennels, each dog showed off their best quality and asked

The lucky ones heard in reply

One by one, Bear's friends left The
shelter and went to their new homes.
The shelter became emptier and quieter.
Bear had mixed feelings.
He was overjoyed for his friends, yet
extremely lonely and sad for himself.

"Why doesn't anyone want me?" frowned poor black, unmemorable
Bear. Snoth looked up at a sad, teary-eyed pup and gave Bear's paw
a big hug.

Bear had asked, "Can I go home with you?" over and over again
just like the others had, but he was passed by each time. The
Room of No Return seemed to be getting closer and closer.

Bear was losing hope and running out of time.

There were only ten minutes remaining until the shelter closed
its doors. With his head hung low, Bear walked back to his rickety
bed and slumped down next to his jaded, furry friend Snoth.
Tired from a long, helpless day, Bear started drifting asleep
to the buzz of the others and their new families rushing out
the door.

Bear dreamt of an endless green field on a cool summer's eve. He and his new family were having a grand picnic with a mountain of peanut butter sandwiches that were made specially for him.

Bear finally felt safe, happy, cared for and free. This must be love! He wanted to stay here and play fetch with his people forever!

Bear was suddenly awoken
by the sound of quiet, shuffling
footsteps. It sounded like they
were coming toward his kennel.
There were only two minutes left showing
on the shelter's rusty wall clock. Poor black, unmemorable Bear
had already been through enough rejections for one day. He
closed his eyes again, wishing to doze back to dreaming of that
lush field and nice things one last time.

The kennel doors rattled gently. Bear's ears perked up, and he turned his boxy head to see a girl—a seemingly unmemorable, normal girl. She, with black hair and a funny, toothy smile, was looking down fondly at Bear. Oddly familiar, thought Bear. The girl quickly knelt down and offered Bear a broken dog treat.

Bear was intrigued. He got up and cautiously approached the girl's open hand. She moved her hand closer in. *Manners*, he reminded himself. Bear did not want to seem too eager or too hyper. He did not want to scare her away.

He politely licked up the treat and chomped on it as gently as he could. At the same time, his tail could not contain the excitement and it wagged up a gust of wind that made Snoth fall over onto his back. *Oh no*, he thought, *did I ruin my chance?* But to his surprise, he heard a giggle.

Bear felt a tug in his little heart. *Be courageous.* With crumbs still stuck to his gums, he looked up at the girl's dark brown eyes to ask, "Can I go—"

"Do you want to come home with me?" the girl interrupted. She smiled her toothy smile again. Bear couldn't believe what his big, floppy ears had just heard. He spun around in a tight circle, grabbed Snoth, and gave a hardy bark of approval. Bear looked into the girl's eyes and she stared back. He felt it. His dreams were going to come true. There would be countless picnics with mountains of peanut butter sandwiches and games of fetch until dusk. They both would never be forgotten. They both would be known and loved forever.

True Stories of our Doggo Friends

Abby (Otter's sister)

Breed: Pug

Found or Adopted: May 2015 from the Seattle Pug Rescue

It all started in 2015 with Steve and Amanda's first pug girl, Baby Bear, also known as B.B. She was a three-year-old pug who had a zest for life. B.B. was given to Amanda and Steven by a friend who was forced to give her up. By December that year, the couple had also adopted Otter. B.B. and Otter had bonded immediately. They fought and loved each other like any other couple would. They spent hours cleaning each other's ears and grooming each other. Their love was cut short.

Three months later, B.B. showed signs of pug dog encephalitis (PDE) out of nowhere. PDE is a rare disease found in pugs. Her own body was attacking her brain and nervous system. Steve and Amanda tried every course of action possible. B.B. was granted only one extra day on this earth. The couple brought Otter to say goodbye. You could tell Otter knew what was going on. After B.B.'s passing, Otter was depressed for a couple of months. So were Steve and Amanda.

Otter would lay by B.B.'s crate when they talked about her. He didn't eat, go for walks, or play like he normally did. Steve and Amanda didn't want to rush into adopting so soon, but Otter's condition was telling them that he needed a buddy by his side. So, they contacted the Seattle Pug Rescue and were told they had the perfect pug girl for them. They went to visit her the week after.

Abby was a senior pug who had two different stints with the rescue. Her previous owner had to relinquish her because the owner wasn't allowed to have animals at her new assisted living home. When Steve and Amanda had sat down on the ground to talk with their SPR contact, this little, petite pug girl climbed and snuggled into their laps. Within five minutes, they knew Abby was going home with them. She was full of love and smiles on the way home. The couple knew that they had made the right choice.

Otter had no objections to a new pug in the home, but it took him a few months to adjust and share his belongings. After about five months, Otter seemed to have realized that Abby was his older sister. He now protects her whenever another dog is mean to her. He respects her space and will not walk over her or bump her out of place. And Abby follows him everywhere, especially on walks where she marks wherever he marks. When Steve and Amanda walk Abby alone, she seems lost without Otter. Now they are inseparable siblings.

THEN AND NOW

Abby now lives in Puyallup, Washington, with her brother, Otter. The two now share each other's personal space. Otter lets Abby lay her head on him with no protest. They comfort each other on car rides. They even try to copy each other's antics. Abby whines when she is impatient or feels left out, and Otter now does this as well. Abby tends to do a handstand pee. Otter has tried it a few times too. We know for sure that Otter loves his older sister because he now does the classic pug slouching position. He had never done that before, even when B.B. was still with the family.

AS WRITTEN BY AMANDA

Abby has brought our family happiness, and gave us a chance to finally heal from the loss of B.B. It still hurts, but Abby has eased the pain and showed us that no matter how old we are, we still should have the same zest for life as we were young. Tomorrow is never promised. As the pugs' parents, we take them out as much as possible and share the world with them. That chance was taken away from us with B.B. Abby has truly been our angel, our savior to continue living and cherish each other to the fullest.

Our love has grown tremendously. From day one, Abby had no walls up. She wanted us to feel and have love once again. Our hearts were still bleeding when B.B. passed, but we knew Otter was hurting much, much more. He knows that Abby has brought his humans happiness, so he now can also feel love again.

Amos

Breed: Mastiff, pit, pony mix

Found or Adopted: July 30, 2016, from Denver, Colorado

In December of 2015, Carisa had to put her dog down. It was the right decision, but she was devastated and had no intention of getting another dog. Even so, Carisa's love for dogs and camping led to her borrowing others' dogs on weekends. She became the Goldilocks of dog borrowers. Some dogs were too small. Some didn't listen. And some barked way too much. Carisa was at her wits' end but still not ready to commit to a dog again. Then entered Amos.

Carisa was in the park in Denver for her birthday. Suddenly, a floppy, wiggly puppy walked by and crawled right into her lap. The alleged owner didn't seem to be paying attention while the puppy had wandered right to the birthday girl. Carisa fell in love immediately. It turned out that the puppy was being fostered and was up for adoption next week.

Carisa spent the whole week trying to convince herself that she didn't need him. She told herself that the puppy wasn't as quiet as he had seemed at the park, that he wasn't as interested in people, that he just loved ambling off, and that he simply wasn't perfect enough. She was a woman possessed with love for this pup. So, the next week she got herself to go to the adoption event, quite sure that she would leave the event without a dog.

But once there, the same puppy from the park crawled right into her lap again, while his littermates barked and chewed on everything around them. He was hers. The pup knew it even if Carisa didn't. Carisa looked into the black pup's eager blue-green eyes. He was perfect. Perfect Amos.

The adoption center said he was four months old and would be about sixty pounds. A year after the adoption, Amos grew to be a solid ninety-pound range dog, and the two have spent almost every weekend camping and hiking since. Amos is even great at stand-up paddleboarding and kayaking. Amos was clearly Carisa's puppy soulmate.

THEN AND NOW

Amos now lives with his mom in Denver, Colorado. Amos and Carisa have been through so much together, especially through their new adventures, camping, and being active.

AS WRITTEN BY CARISA

Amos has taught me the importance of meeting every day as a new adventure, and the power of forgiveness. That's Amos! Two months after Amos came home with me, the other dog in the house bit him for climbing in the crate with him. Amos almost lost an eye then. About three months after that incident, they were snuggling together in the same crate and became best friends. That's Amos! He doesn't quit until everyone around him loves him. He is the reason I can keep facing the world alone, and I can't think of anyone I would rather have with me. Likewise, Amos will try anything just so he can stay by my side, even sailing! That's Amos!

Annabelle (Annie)

Breed: Border collie

Found or Adopted:
November 22, 2016, from a rescue in Washington, New Jersey

When Gillian first saw the picture of Annabelle (Annie) on Facebook, she immediately thought, Oh my, she is so beautiful! At the same time, she zoomed in and looked at the dog's eyes. Annie looked terrified. It was almost certain that she was afraid and didn't trust anyone. Gillian felt like something was pulling her to Annie. She just knew she was the one. Gillian felt that she had to be the one to teach her how to love and to trust again.

Kent and Gillian decided in the summer of 2016 that they were going to start looking for a dog. Kent's mom was putting their house up for sale and Gillian's mom was fighting a deadly battle with Stage IV small cell lung cancer. The couple needed something more—something to take care of, something to love. They had no clue which breed they wanted to adopt, so Gillian searched and followed a ton of local rescues on Facebook.

It wasn't until the middle of November when she finally saw a beautiful dog, Annie, on a rescue's post. Annie looked so sad on the foster home's kitchen floor. Gillian took a screenshot of the post and sent it to her boyfriend. She knew right there and then that she would be part of their family no matter what it took to get her. Gillian got in contact with the rescue and set up a meeting.

Gillian and Kent took Kipper, their thirteen-year old long-haired toy Chihuahua to the meet. Kipper wasn't too keen about Annie, but Kent and Gillian immediately fell in love with her. Knowing Kent's mom was on vacation and they were looking to move out, the couple took Annie back inside to her foster's home and stepped out separately onto the porch to decide what they were going to do. They both looked at each other and knew the other's answer. It was a yes.

They walked back in, knelt down, and Gillian asked Annabelle if she was ready to finally go home. Her eyes lit up brighter than the lights on a Christmas tree, and then there was the butt wiggle. It was a yes from Annie. They signed the papers that day and set up a time to pick her up two days later. This was because Annie had grown attached to the foster home's youngest daughter, so Gillian wanted to make sure that they had proper closure before taking Annie home.

Gillian had asked about Annie's story. Annie had been through so much in her short life of only two years. Originally from Georgia, Annie was found by the rescue. When the rescue folks drove down to get her, they said she was roaming the streets by herself, with no one to love and show her how to have a good life. Her hair was matted and she didn't trust people because she had been abused. It was possible her previous owners had physically abused her to the point where she couldn't trust people, especially men. Annie's story before that is unconfirmed, but the suspicions as to why she was afraid of new people was that Annie was most likely abused and left on the street to die. The rescue went down and brought her back to New Jersey. They had adopted her out to an older gentleman who unfortunately had passed away due to a heart attack. So, the family brought Annie back to the rescue. Annie had no idea of the love she was about to receive when Gillian found her ad online.

Two days passed. Kent and Gillian drove down the highway to pick up their newest family member. They had gotten Annie a pink camouflage leash and harness, and of course, a plush duck for her to play with on the way home. As soon as they pulled into the driveway, Gillian could hear Annie barking from inside the house. They opened the door and she came flying out to greet them. It was like Annie knew it was her time to finally go home. Kent and Gillian loaded her in the car and said their goodbyes. Before they got back onto the highway, Annie had completely destroyed the brand-new toy they had gotten her. Annie gave both Kent and Gillian never-ending kisses and fell asleep in Gillian's lap.

THEN AND NOW

Annie currently lives with her mom and dad in Stroudsburg, Pennsylvania, but longs for a trip to Arizona. A month after they brought Annie home, they had to make an emergency vet visit and feared the worst. Their hearts dropped when the test results came back. Annie had Parvovirus*. Because they noticed it early on, she was given the necessary treatment and within a month and a half, she was back to being her normal, happy self. Later, Annie welcomed a little sister, Skylar, a two-month-old Border collie, to the family in October 2018. Annie and Skye are inseparable to this day. They love playing in the snow, going to the puppy park, and ripping apart plush toys together.

AS WRITTEN BY GILLIAN

I never knew how much I could possibly love an animal until I met Annie. It didn't take long for her to warm up to us. My mom passed away in February 2017. Annie never left my side when I was upset. She cried with me. She cuddled me when I needed her the most. She was the best friend I had been searching for all my life. To this day, she and I are inseparable. She loves going for car rides, waiting patiently by the door for Kent to come home from work, and playing in the snow.

Add as Footnote: *According to caninejournal.com, the mortality rate in dogs with Parvovirus is 90 percent if left untreated, and 5–20 percent if aggressively treated. Around 80 percent of adult dogs do not show symptoms, and puppies are most susceptible. Dogs can show symptoms between three and ten days after being exposed.

Bentley

Breed: Pitbull

Found or Adopted:
March 15, 2016, from an abusive home in Lancaster, Pennsylvania

Sarah really wasn't looking for a dog. Bentley just kind of "happened." Someone said they knew of someone getting rid of a pit bull who was in need, and Sarah couldn't say no after she saw his face. When the previous owners dropped Bentley off at Sarah's home, they just pushed him out of the car. They didn't even say hello to Sarah or goodbye to Bentley. And that was the last Sarah saw of them.

Bentley was only twenty pounds heavy. His neck was scarred and scabby with pieces of rope still stuck in it. The vet later told Sarah that Bentley must have been tied up outside for a long time with a rope so tight that it got embedded into his neck. When Bentley first came into Sarah's house, his tail was tucked and he had fear in his eyes. He was scared to let Sarah touch him. Sarah cried. Sarah was diagnosed with bipolar disorder, and she had been having a tough time coping the past few months.

Just as Sarah saved Bentley, Bentley also helped change Sarah drastically. Whenever Sarah cried or screamed, Bentley just lay with her. Sarah couldn't believe that this abused, broken-down dog could still love her. She felt so imperfect, and yet all Bentley ever wanted was to lie with her and feel a gentle hand. Bentley has grown so much since then, but he will forever be afraid of men. Sarah hopes one day he will get past that fear. She says she is forever in his debt, and that he really did save her life.

THEN AND NOW

Bentley now lives in Elizabethtown, Pennsylvania.

AS WRITTEN BY SARAH

Since I first got Bentley, we've been working on many things. Since he was tied up outside, he had no house manners. He now knows how to sit, lay down, give his paws, roll over, and stay. He also goes to the door when he wants to go out, and even carries his leash to the door when he wants to be walked. For me, he's become my coping mechanism. If I ever feel depressed, he can tell. He'll follow me around the house until I cry and then he just sits with me.

Django (Jjanggoo)

Breed: Border collie/blue heeler

Found or Adopted: May 2017 from abusive owners in Everett, Washington

'Django was a Craigslist dog. For months, Jan had looked at numerous shelters and foster homes to adopt a dog but was rejected because she and her husband, Brandon, lived in an apartment. Jan was almost out of hope, but decided to take a look at Craigslist. She was looking for a cattle dog, specifically a blue heeler. Finally, in May 2017, she came across Django's ad online. Jan and her husband, Brandon, were instantly sold and made arrangements to pick Django up the next day. Django's previous owner said she wanted to rehome him because she was pregnant and her husband was being deployed.

Once Jan and Brandon brought Django home, they began to realize the dog's habits and mannerisms were very unusual and alarming. Around nine o'clock at night, Django would become very defensive and growl intensely if they got too close or touched him. This happened every night, and Django would go straight to a dark corner. Jan figured that the behavior Django was displaying was because he was in a new environment, surrounded by two completely new faces.

As the months progressed, the strange behavior continued every night, like clockwork. Jan and Brandon began to suspect that the odd habits were not due to the newness of his home, but perhaps because he was conditioned to defend himself. Django's new, worried parents asked other dog owners who had also adopted to see if they experienced similar behaviors. Upon hearing Django's story, the others agreed that his mannerisms were abnormal, and that Django was possibly abused into going to bed at a certain time, and perhaps even tossed and locked in a dark room until morning came.

The new parents also discovered that Django would react to hand movements by closing his eyes as if he was ready to be swatted. It was quite a heartbreaking realization that their new pup had been abused. The

couple began to change the way they interacted withDjango by reinforcing favorable behaviors with treats and praises. For example, when Django would growl out of the blue, he was reassured that he was safe, with gentle pets and some treats. Eventually, his personality began to change and he grew more and more accustomed to affection, even begging for cuddles and head kisses. After months of training and extra love, Django has now become a completely different dog from what he was when he was first brought home!

Django isn't a very "dog-social" dog; his best friends are his ball and his humans. But he is also not aggressive or confrontational to other dogs that he meets at the park or on the street. He loves all people and will push his butt onto his human friends for a good butt rub. He is through and through just a very happy and curious dog!

THEN AND NOW

Django now lives with his mom and dad in downtown Seattle, Washington. He helps his mom bake delicious floral buttercream cakes and loves to play fetch. But his favorite hobby is being a cuddle-monster.

AS WRITTEN BY JAN

To be completely honest, I had a hard time bonding with Django and had a little bit of adoption remorse because his growling scared me and I didn't know how to handle his mood swings at times. But, now that I've established boundaries with him and now that he knows I am in charge of HIM, he is a very obedient, loyal, and loving dog. His derpiness makes it easy for me to make fun of him, but he doesn't know the difference, and he ALWAYS needs to follow us around and touch us in some way while we are just relaxing. At times it can get annoying, but most of the time it is endearing to know that someone loves your company no matter what. Django teaches me so much about how to love unconditionally.

Dolly

Breed: Chihuahua mix

Found or Adopted: November 21, 2016, from the Regional Animal Services
of King County (RASKC) adoption center at the Petco in Kirkland, Washington

Sophie and Robert had been considering adopting a dog for quite some time before they found Dolly. Sophie had been searching on rescue websites for almost a year when she saw a picture of Dolly, formerly known as Twinkle. The picture on the RASKC website showed her in a little sweater. Sophie instantly fell in love with Dolly's huge, adorable ears. The description read that she was social, so the couple decided to go meet Dolly.

When Sophie and Robert met Dolly, they sat down with her. She was so tiny—only 3 lb, to be exact. Despite her size, Dolly had no fear. She immediately jumped into their laps and licked their noses with her long tongue. There were some other sweet little pups available at the shelter, but Sophie and Robert kept coming back to their first choice because of her impressionable temperament.

Undecided, the couple walked around the shelter to talk it through. Robert was afraid he would accidentally, fatally step on her because she was so tiny. They kept hesitating, so they eventually went home. In the car ride home, Sophie and Robert realized that if Dolly's size was the only thing holding them back, then they had to go back for her the next day. She was perfect in every other way.

The next day, when the decided couple got there, they looked through the window and Dolly was still there. They were so relieved and happy. Sophie walked over to the desk where an RASKC officer was helping another woman. Sophie saw a folder on the desk with "Twinkle" written on the top. Her heart sank.

"Are you adopting Twinkle?!" Sophie asked with desperation in her voice. She was sincerely hoping for the woman to say no.

The woman turned around with a worried look, and said, "Yeah... why?"

Sophie stopped herself and reassured the woman, "No, no, she is amazing... Such a sweet dog."

Robert and Sophie were so sad they had missed out but decided that the next time they find the perfect dog, they wouldn't hesitate.

A week later, Sophie was perusing the rescue sites again, and there was Twinkle!

"Twinkle's back! This has to be a mistake. We have to go see tomorrow!"

The next day after work, Sophie and Robert both raced over to the RASKC adoption center. And it was true. Twinkle was back!

Sophie immediately interrogated them, "What happened? Did the adopter have cats and it didn't go well? Why would someone bring her back?"

Apparently, it just wasn't a good fit. The excited couple was given a second chance, and they did not hesitate this time. They adopted her and changed her name to Dolly, after Dolly Parton, an American star with a big personality. Dolly continues to be the shining star in their lives.

THEN AND NOW

Dolly currently lives with her humans (Robert and Sophie) and her somewhat annoying kitty siblings (Gin and Abby) in Redmond, Washington. Sophie cannot begin to explain how much more she loves Dolly now. Dolly has gained a healthy pound since they rescued her, but everyone still thinks she is a puppy. They had to figure out food sensitivities and other issues at first, but have now switched her to a raw diet, and Dolly has never been healthier! Her favorite treats include celery, blueberries, carrots, and watermelon. The family now occasionally fosters small dogs and Dolly loves to meet and take care of the other little ones in need. Dolly has learned a couple of tricks, such as "touch" and "spin," and she loves to go everywhere with Sophie and Robert. She is a fair-weather dog, so her best friends are the heater, the sun, and her favorite toy, a crinkly, squeaky peppermint. She has had that toy since her first winter with her family, and it will always be her very favorite. Dolly has truly completed their family.

Duke

Breed: Unknown mixed breed

Found or Adopted: February 16, 2013, from the Bermuda SPCA

When Nadia lost her beloved boxer pup in December 2012 to juvenile kidney disease, it broke her heart. She knew that she wasn't ready for another pup, and she didn't know when she would be. Nadia also knew that even getting a purebred puppy from a top-rated kennel was not a guarantee of getting a healthy dog. Having learned the hard way that even "good" breeders indulge in bad practices for interbreeding, Nadia knew that her next pup would almost certainly be a rescue. After making the decision to donate most of her late boxer's belongings to the Bermuda SPCA, Nadia decided to put herself down on the list for a possible rescue dog and trust the universe with the timing. Knowing that most people would be looking for a smaller dog, she put everything down on her wish list for a dog that she knew most people wouldn't want: big, bouncy, high-energy—you get the idea!

In Bermuda, it is very hard to get a rescue dog because most of the dogs, especially the pit bull type, are picked up by government dog wardens and euthanized. Luckily for Duke and his sister, the Government Dog Warden and the Bermuda SPCA Inspector persuaded their original owner to surrender both of them to the SPCA. Fortunately, due to their Labrador looks, they were classified as Labrador mixes, which meant that the Bermuda SPCA were free to take, rehabilitate, and rehome them.

At the time, the two dog siblings were in a very bad condition. They were emotionally neglected and in a poor physical state because they did not have enough food, and were also having bad cases of mange.

A couple of months later, on Nadia's birthday, she got a call from the Bermuda SPCA. "We think we have a match for you!"

Nadia was still grieving the loss of her boxer, but because of the timing, she felt that this was nothing short of divine intervention. So she went on her way to meet Duke for the first time, who was called Taco at the time.

The first time she met Duke, Nadia wasn't sure what to feel or think. She suspected that he was in the same boat as her. While Nadia was still grieving the loss of her boxer, Duke was grieving the loss of his sister.

The two did not connect immediately. Nadia spent some time with Duke in the outside run at the SPCA. Duke jumped a lot on Nadia, but he seemed to figure out quickly that when she turned her back on him, the best way to get her attention was to be polite.

A day or two later, Nadia went back for a second visit, and this time she took her best friend along. Duke and Nadia connected immediately this time. Nadia felt like she should not be leaving him there, and made the firm decision to adopt him. At the time, Duke was on antibiotics and was still being treated for mange and tummy troubles. Nadia went to her local animal feed store and picked up some really good food for him which would help with his tummy. She gave it to the SPCA so that they could slowly wean him onto the new diet. This way, Duke could be good by the time he came to Nadia's home.

Two days after Valentine's Day of 2019, Duke went home with Nadia. Nadia was nervous about how Duke would be in the car, but he seemed to know that this was a good thing, so he was an absolute angel during the short ride home.

It was a different story when they entered the house. Duke immediately barked madly and lunged at one of Nadia's cats. (It was her lovely brown tabby called Teddy, who later became Duke's best buddy!) Duke was left outside while Nadia grabbed her sneakers, and then they went on a very long walk before trying again to introduce Duke to his new feline brothers. The second time, Duke was a little better but still didn't quite know how to behave around the kitties.

Spoiler alert: Crate training was a godsend. Nadia was forever grateful that the SPCA had started this training with Duke before he came home with her. Using the crate, a bedsheet, and treats, just a day and a half later Duke was able to be free in the house with the cats. He was never aggressive toward his new family members, but he just hadn't ever learned how to be inside a house and behave appropriately with other animals.

Even with all the love and care from the Bermuda SPCA, Duke was still skinny when he came home the first day. But eventually, Duke started to put on weight, and although he'd never been a heavy dog, it made Nadia extremely happy that his ribs were no longer visible. Duke's heart was always in the right place, and because he was such a smart pup, he learned everything quickly. Positive reinforcement was like magic, and it built his confidence. It took some time, but Duke became more confident with each passing day. After only one week, he had learned to be discerning and not bark at everyone who went past the house. He was good as gold and a real pleasure to train and work with.

THEN AND NOW

Duke and Nadia have moved from Devonshire Parish, Bermuda, to the UK and are having a new adventure together. There is not a day that goes by that Nadia is not extremely grateful for having had the good fortune to adopt Duke. He truly is her best friend and her family. She is privileged for being able to take him to work with her, and almost all of her clients are dog-friendly people who love him to pieces, too!

AS WRITTEN BY NADIA

Everyone talks about rescuing pups. The simple truth is that they rescue you. They make you a better person. They are unwavering in their loyalty and affection, and they keep you healthy by encouraging you to get out and about, especially when you might not feel like it!

Trust is not something that you can fast forward. It took some time for Duke to trust me fully, and I think that is because it took him some time to feel more confident in himself. With his greater confidence came a greater sense of cheekiness and naughtiness, too. I LOVE the fact that he literally speaks his mind. He is quite vocal, but smart enough to know when it's not the right time to vocalize.

When I had problems with Duke's confidence in the early days, I reached out to a local dog trainer who trained him when he was at the SPCA. Having her as a resource was invaluable. When you adopt an animal, you adopt their past. This shouldn't be intimidating. It's like anything else in life: there is absolutely no shame in asking for help, and the rewards of doing so are most certainly worth it!

Gracie

Breed: Rottweiler

Found or Adopted: December 2014 from the Everett Animal Shelter

James and Mallory had wanted to adopt a rescue dog for quite a while. They had visited all the shelters in a thirty-mile radius from their home. They did this every weekend and fell in love with many dogs. However, they were rejected over and over again because they lived in an apartment. The couple was at a loss and thought they would never get to adopt.

Then one day, they moved to a new house and immediately went to the Everett Animal Shelter! As they walked up and down the aisles, James and Mallory both stopped when they saw Gracie. She was adorable! They fell in love, filled out the application, and got to do a meet-and-greet.

Gracie was a little intense. As they came to find out, Gracie was a stray who had been found on the side of the road and picked up by animal control. The shelter said that Gracie most likely came from a home that kept her as an outside dog only. When Gracie was first brought into the shelter, she could not walk on the floors because she was so used to only walking on grass and dirt. The concrete flooring was so weird to her that she just kept slipping.

Even at 75 lb, Gracie was very underweight, as dirty as can be, and her nails had grown out considerably. She also wasn't potty-trained even at the age of 1.5 years. The shelter told the new parents that Gracie would be a lot of work, but if they were patient with her, she would turn out to be the most loyal and loving dog.

The determined couple decided to take on the challenge.

Neither of them knew just how difficult the next six months were actually going to be. When they brought Gracie home, the dog had bad manners. She tried to dig holes in the carpet, and jumped on their tables and counters with all four paws. Mallory even took time off work to stay with Gracie, because when left alone, Gracie would chew up the couch and poop on the carpet.

After months of hard work, Grace was finally potty-trained! She slowly started to adapt, and James and Mallory could actually watch TV again. (Gracie believed everything she saw on the screen was real and would bark at it uncontrollably and try to knock the TV over.) She has grown into such a loving, cuddly, protective, loyal companion. Mallory and James are so grateful for being rejected by the other places because otherwise they would never have been able to bring their wonderful Gracie home!

THEN AND NOW

Gracie now lives in Lynnwood, Washington. Mallory treats Gracie like she were her own child. Their relationship at first was hard, of course, but Mallory stayed patient with Gracie, and worked with her to get her to be the wonderful dog she is today!

Gypsy

Breed: Saluki, Dutch shepherd, and coonhound mix

Found or Adopted: October 1, 2016, from Loved at Last Dog Rescue in Iran

Five months after their dog had passed, Amanda and her husband, Joseph, knew they were ready to adopt again. They searched on PetFinder.com and looked through local animal shelters, but were surprised that they were not able to find their new dog within the first day. After another search, Amanda finally found Gypsy on PetFinder. Gypsy had been living with a foster family in British Columbia for three weeks by this time.

The adoption was through a group she had never heard of before, named Loved at Last Dog Rescue. The dog on the screen that had stolen Amanda's heart was an Iranian street dog. Gypsy's description wasn't very detailed; it simply stated that she was sweet and that her leg had been hurt while living in Iran. Amanda wasn't particularly looking for a dog from a foreign country, but the more she read about dogs from Iran, her heart melted. She pushed back tears from her eyes while she read the details of how different life was for dogs in Iran than in the U.S. She read that in Iran, dogs were discarded, mistreated, and that it was nearly illegal to own dogs there.

Amanda knew she wanted to rescue this darling girl. Thankfully, Amanda worked from home and she could be with her new dog consistently. Many factors played into Amanda and Joseph's successful application: working from home, living in a quiet neighborhood, and having a large fenced-in yard. Despite the many applicants, Amanda and Joseph got the call that they were picked to be Gypsy's new family!

It was obvious from the videos that Amanda received from Gypsy's foster mom that the dog had a damaged leg, but that didn't stop their excitement. The couple knew they could get their newest family member the right treatment. They were just so thankful that Gypsy was no longer a street dog in Iran.

A few days later, the dog-parents-to-be drove up to British Columbia, and just hours later, they were united with Gypsy. Amanda recalled that Gypsy was sweet, a little timid, and very skinny (fifteen pounds underweight, to be exact), but she was regal. The handoff was bittersweet because you could tell that the foster family truly cared for her. Gypsy did great in the car, although she was a little nervous at first. She slept most of the way home. Amanda kept looking back and saying how sweet and pretty she was.

THEN AND NOW

Gypsy now lives in Edmonds, Washington, with her parents and her foster brother, Alexi, who is also from Iran. For a year, Amanda and Joseph waited to see how Gypsy would do with her exercises and a custom-made brace for her injured rear left leg. However, her arthritis got much worse, and she started guarding her injured leg while around other dogs. And so, in 2018, the decision was made to amputate that leg. Gypsy recovered well, as she was previously used to only using three legs. She is a much happier dog now!

Amanda and Joseph always get compliments on how fast and agile their dog is "even for only having three legs." Gypsy is almost always still the fastest dog at the dog park, due to the part-saluki blood. Gypsy also loves the beach, mostly for running and digging. She will happily go into the water, but only up to her belly and absolutely no further. Her scent drive is incredibly strong and she loves to tunnel through tall grass, snow, and fields of brush. Along with their new addition, Alexi, they are a happy family.

AS WRITTEN BY AMANDA

Since Gypsy's first day, she has bonded to both myself and Joseph. It took Gypsy days to go up and down our stairs and to get used to being walked on a leash. Now Gypsy knows the leash is always associated with a great thing! The first time I walked her, two dogs were walking by our front driveway. Gypsy bolted back behind some large rocks and started shaking. I quickly discovered she was terrified of other dogs. We kept walking, but then she hid in a ditch when she saw a dog from 50 feet away. It took me sitting with her, talking to her, and making sure no other dogs were around until she finally came out.

Each week she did progress. She started to sit when she saw other dogs, which we learned is a calming signal. Now she can go to the dog park without being scared. We quickly realized she loves smaller dogs. While she will play with some dogs her size, she really enjoys playing chase with smaller dogs, her favorite playmates. She loves her toys and enjoys her short training sessions. She loves people, our morning cuddles, her small squeaky red ball, walking on trails, and playing in the sand. She's made so much progress, it makes my heart melt.

Now we have a new addition, Alexi, who is also from Iran. He desperately needed to get into the States to start rehab, so I am fostering him. He is a 20-pound terrier mix who came to us fully paralyzed (not able to sit, stand or walk on his own). Six months after countless rehab appointments, acupuncture, laser, Chinese herbs, homeopathic remedies and osteopathy, he took his first steps by himself, using his rear legs in his quad cart! It's a slow but steady process, and we're currently trying to wake up his front legs and continue to get his muscles stronger.

Gypsy and Alexi bonded right away, and they have their own unique way of playing together. I go on walks with my tripod dog and my paralyzed dog in my backpack, and we always get a lot of questions. I think it's so important to teach kindness and compassion, and that even creatures who are special, who need that patience and love, really matter.

Lucy

Breed: Miniature schnauzer

Found or Adopted: September 16, 2017, from Tracy's Dog in San Antonio, Texas

Emily and her family had previously adopted a miniature schnauzer named Frost, who was also a rescue and whom they had for ten years. Frost passed away from heart disease in April 2017. From their experience with Frost, Emily and her family had decided that they would always adopt from a rescue rather than buy a dog from a pet store. Heartbroken from the loss, the family needed time to think about the next step.

Emily's husband was online, looking at different rescue organizations, and found Tracy's Dogs. Lucy, who was named Chelsie at the time, was the first and only dog Emily looked at. She was a purebred miniature schnauzer that was around ten months old. Emily showed the picture of Lucy to her husband and children and they sent in the application that night! Emily knew she had to have her, and she knew they would change her name to Lucy, after Emily's grandmother.

They waited for about a week to hear back from Tracy's Dogs. After a thorough vetting process, including phone interviews and reference checks, the family was approved for adoption. The process for adoption was not scary, but it was just nerve-racking waiting for that call. And they had to wait for about three weeks for the shelter to make the trip up with Lucy and the other dogs. They learned through the phone interviews that Lucy had been dropped off at a high kill shelter by her previous owner because she needed too much attention.

On September 16, 2017, the family traveled to a PetSmart store in Secaucus, New Jersey, to pick up Lucy. This was during Hurricane Harvey. Lucy and around forty-eight other dogs were transported from San Antonio, Texas, in a trailer by the staff members from Tracy's Dogs. The trip took a total of thirty-six hours. Emily and the family waited with over a hundred people who were also waiting for their dogs. It was even posted live on Tracy's Dogs' Facebook. During the car ride, Lucy was scared and Emily's daughter held her for the entire one and half hour car ride up to New York, finally bringing Lucy back to safety forever.

THEN AND NOW

Lucy lives in Dutchess County, New York, and has become a certified therapy dog. When Lucy first got home, she didn't know how to walk up the stairs, and she was very scared to go into the other rooms in the house. She would stretch her front legs out to look around the doors until she felt safe. Lucy wouldn't leave her bed (Emily doesn't even think she had one of her own before) for a couple of days. She warmed up pretty fast after that, and now Lucy loves running around and exploring the house. She loves everyone she meets and is so happy and friendly. Emily can't imagine her previous owner putting her in a kill shelter saying she needed too much attention! Lucy also has a new brother, Ozzy, who was also adopted out of the same rescue, and they are happily living their life's greatest adventure together.

Luna

Breed: Unknown (possibly Catahoula leopard dog, boxer, greyhound mix)

Found or Adopted:
April 29, 2017, from DAWGS Prison Program in Pottsville, Pennsylvania

Both of Luna's parents grew up with dogs. After they got married, Jenna and Tyler knew that adopting a dog was the first thing they wanted to do. They searched and searched. They applied for a number of dogs through multiple rescue agencies, but it took almost a year before they found Luna. The couple had a number of interviews and home visits and were approved a few times, but it never seemed to work out for various reasons that would break your heart.

Since Jenna was a pediatric psychologist, she was looking for a pup that would also have a good temperament for a possible therapy dog. As fate would have it, Luna's short bio said just that! Tyler went to meet Luna at DAWGS Prison Program and fell in love. "The purpose of this program is to rescue dogs from shelters, place them in a training program, and then adopt them out to their forever homes. In an effort to give them a second chance at life, the dogs are paired up with inmates at Three Local Prisons. They provide the dogs with basic obedience training, socialization, and love. A very strict screening process is utilized when selecting both dog and inmate to ensure that a positive result is made. The inmates learn from professional trainers to teach their partnering dog basic obedience commands such as sit, stay, down, heal, and various other basic commands over a period of 4 to 6 weeks. The dogs live with the inmates 24/7, where they will learn how to socialize with other individuals and be provided with a routine of eating, crating, and toilet training. At the conclusion of their training, the dogs will remain with their partnering inmates until they find their forever home." (Description taken from Facebook)

Luna spent four weeks there learning basic commands, such as sit, wait, and heel. She was also socialized, house-broken, and crate-trained. After meeting Luna, Tyler came home and told Jenna, "I think she would be the perfect dog for us!"

They both went to meet Luna, hoping the foster dog would pick them. To their relief and joy, Luna came up and wiggled her little booty and snuggled with them right away. Tyler and Jenna took their dog home that night. Luna was very cautious at first, but after a few days of being encouraged to snuggle with her new parents on the couch, she found her perfect spot and seemed to relax. Jenna turned to her husband that night and smiled, "My heart hurts!" They've been a happy little family ever since.

THEN AND NOW

Now living in Hershey, Pennsylvania, Luna is living a wonderful life with her parents. Tyler and Jenna were ready to love Luna from the start, and after she settled into their home and figured out what the rules were, she started to snuggle consistently. It took Luna a few months to get comfortable and really come into her own personality. Watching her grow from cautious to curious was also a process of watching her learn to trust. She always looks at her parents for permission before doing something new, like jumping on the couch at a new place or sniffing a toad. If she gets hurt playing or is afraid of something, she will run barreling toward them for protection.

Luna's problem-solving skills have grown immensely! Jenna says that it is so amazing to watch her figure things out on her own, like how to get a ball out from under the couch. They did a training course with her, and that really allowed her to shine. Luna was super-smart and eager to please, incredibly well-behaved, and so much fun to play with! She can play off leash, and loves to explore new places on hikes and other adventures.

Her first birthday party with her friends was adorable. They got a dog-friendly cake and party hats, and all the dogs went to town! When Luna is happy or excited, her little ears still go doot doot doot and flap while she walks. She also stands on her hind legs and hops like a kangaroo, or spins in a tight little circle. One time she even howled in her sleep! Like any good dog mom, Jenna has thousands of photos of Luna. Tyler and Jenna can't imagine their family without her.

AS WRITTEN BY JENNA

Luna has transformed into quite the independent lady. She loves rough-housing with her dog furiends, especially big dogs, but she is also totally content to just play fetch even if they are around. She gets hyper focused on the ball and always goes into a "point." She is super fast! We take her running with us and she absolutely loves it.

We completed the Canine Good Citizen course and Luna passed her test on the first try. Luna is officially registered as a CGG with the AKC as "Galaxy Eyed Luna the Sass Queen." She is currently in the process of becoming a registered therapy dog with an organization called KPETS that visits all manner of locations. I'm most excited for her to do the children's reading program, where she will sit with children struggling to read as they practice reading story books aloud to her. I have since changed my job and am now a college professor. Luna comes to work with me and is well loved on campus! We also purchased our first home, so Luna finally has a yard of her own to play in! In the living room there's a giant window with a chaise lounge in front, and that's her favorite spot in the house. We're hoping to add another rescue to the family soon.

Miles

Breed: Labrador, pit bull mix

Found or Adopted: Wright Way Rescue in Chicago, Illinois

Matt and Becky had just moved in together into a tiny apartment in Chicago. However, after seeing a photo of two-month-old Miles, they were determined to adopt him. According to Wright Way Rescue, the puppy had been thrown out of a car in Tennessee. A high kill shelter found him and that's when Wright Way took Miles in. Miles spent two weeks at their medical center in Southern Illinois before being transferred to their Chicago adoption center.

The adoption process was fairly easy. They filled out the paperwork and met Miles a few days later. A worker brought the eight-pound puppy out to the caged area. Miles was shaking and absolutely afraid of everything. He leaned against the cage and would not move for anything. Becky's heart broke then and there, and it took everything she had not to cry. How could anyone do this to a poor puppy? she thought. Becky knew they were getting Miles as soon as they had seen his picture, but after meeting him in person, she was determined not to leave that building unless he was coming with her.

With Miles in her arms and walking out the rescue's door, Becky couldn't believe they just gave him to them. In the car ride home, Becky made Matt drive super slow and safe. She never wanted anything bad to happen to Miles again.

The next day, they headed to Minnesota to see Becky's family. It was an eight-hour drive. At this point, Miles still hadn't warmed up to his new family. He would find the smallest corners to hide in at the apartment and almost got stuck behind the toilet at one point. He only ate his food if he was in a corner and would try to dart under cars during walks. During the drive to Minnesota, they stopped to let Miles out in the grass.

Becky tried to run around with Miles, and for the first time he acted like a real puppy! It was barely a glimpse, but nothing made the new parents happier at that moment.

Becky came from a big family with Great Danes, so she was worried the puppy would be overwhelmed once they arrived at the house in Minnesota. However, Miles acted more like a puppy than they had ever seen. He was chasing balls and pouncing around with his paws like puppies do! From then on, he was energetic and happy and it was really wonderful.

THEN AND NOW

Now living in Seattle, Miles is living his best life with his older sister, Dipper. You would absolutely not recognize the dog he is today if you met him as a puppy. His family takes him on a lot of hikes and he has to say hi to everyone! Matt and Becky thought they were going to have problems socializing him, but definitely not. They trained him, and it was incredibly rewarding to watch him sit, shake, and lie down for the first time. At first, Becky worked from home and they would listen to music together and spend their days at the park. He met kids and fell in love with strollers, insisting on smelling and meeting the babies. He is one of the most trusting dogs now. After getting his sister, Dipper, he's been incredibly helpful in the transition. While jealous at first, he helps to make sure she behaves. With both of them, we can leave them free and they don't touch anything and that credit goes to Miles. The dog who was once afraid of everything helped Dipper feel welcome and safe when she was afraid. In August 2019, Miles and Dipper were a special part of their parents' wedding, even wearing flower crowns on their heads!

Moxie

Breed: Pitbull

Found or Adopted:
Oct 30, 2008, running down 124th street in Kirkland

In 2008, Nikki found Moxie running down the street in Kirkland, Washington. After picking her up, their first car ride was to the grooming salon where Nikki worked. Moxie was covered with fleas like something from a horror movie. There was also a lot of blood and puss on the right side of her face. Nikki bathed Moxie and took her home. At that time, Nikki was moving houses, so Moxie rode on top of boxes all the way home.

Nikki and her fiancé already had three dogs of their own, so they decided to adopt Moxie out to another family. Because Moxie had been terrified of people and would run from them, after about a year of socialization training, she was ready to be adopted to another family. Although she was still a little nervous around people, her training had helped her become more of a social butterfly.

Moxie was finally adopted by a family—a family that returned her four days later. This made Moxie afraid of people again. It took another four months of helping Moxie feel confident and safe again. Right around the time Moxie was better, it was Nikki's birthday. Nikki told her fiancé during their grocery shopping that the only thing she wanted for her special day was Moxie. She almost cried thinking about it. Her fiancé said okay. And it was happily ever after for Moxie and Nikki.

THEN AND NOW

Moxie lives in Redmond, Washington, as a therapy dog who works with soldiers, children in hospitals, and mothers that have just given birth. She is also Nikki's personal service dog and has helped her get past her PTSD. Moxie had a spinal aneurysm in 2016 that left her paralyzed for a month. Moxie did water therapy and worked with a physical therapist for six months after the surgery. Now Moxie not only walks, but also runs, swims, plays fetch, and spreads joy to others!

Nona

Breed: Siberian husky

Found or Adopted:
March 2, 2013, from Miami-Dade Adoption Center in Florida

Solange never intended to get a dog. She and her mother had been struggling with Solange's mental disorders, medication, and paying off doctor fees. One day in March of 2013, Solange was by the Miami-Dade County Adoption Center and decided to look at the dogs with her sister. The family had just come from a doctor's appointment where it was suggested that because the medication was no longer working, Solange should get a service dog for her issues.

The sisters passed by a few dogs when Solange laid eyes on a sleeping beauty. Nona, a Husky puppy, woke up and gave Solange an angry look. Nona had face markings that made her look grumpy, and a sash on her neck that looked like a wave crashing down into the ocean, which was perfectly cute. The little puppy was four months old at the time with no interest in the other humans other than Solange. Nona also seemed to have an amazing temperament. It was love at first sight for Solange and Nona, feeling right and meant to be.

Solange's sister ran to tell their mother. The sisters managed to convince their mother, who filled out the application. And within a few hours, the family was taking the puppy home. Car rides for Solange were very stressful. However, Nona curled up on her lap and Solange felt a beautiful relaxing wave pass over her. And thus began Nona's life as a working canine.

THEN AND NOW

Nona lives with her mom in Kendall, Florida. Their little family has grown and will continue to grow. Nona now has a younger brother named Champ, a pointer, and as early as 2020, they will be expecting an eight-week old pup named Nox. Nox will be Nona's successor and will learn a cardiac task so that Nona can retire to pet life.

AS WRITTEN BY SOLANGE

As a disabled person my pup has been my lifeline. Our bond has never been stronger. Nona absolutely loves service work. At first it was hard training her basic obedience, however once she had that down, she picked up tasks super fast and she was alerting me to increased heart rates within a week. Every year I've had her has gotten even better.

Oliver Drew (Oli)

Breed: Unknown

Found or Adopted: December 12, 2010, from Daegu, South Korea

Caroline, who had been involved in animal rescue in South Korea, had recently lost her beloved rescue kitten. In her heartbreak, she knew that she wanted to help another soul in need. She decided to visit a shelter that was finding homes for animals before the brutal Korean winter. Caroline found a shelter that was accessible by high speed train about an hour and a half north of her city. Her partner, Megan, although still very heartbroken over the loss of their kitten, agreed to be open-minded and go with her.

When they arrived, the state of the shelter was too much for Megan to bear. She had to go outside to wait for Caroline. This shelter was not even one of the rougher shelters in South Korea, but it was still hard to witness. There were rows and rows of very small wired cages, stacked with more cages on top, three to four cages high. The dogs were standing directly on the wired frames in very dirty cages. All of the dogs in this room were small breeds. The noise of the desperate dogs was deafening.

Caroline steeled herself to look into the eyes of all of the dogs and wrestled with how she would know which soul to rescue. She went to the last row against the far back wall and decided to slowly work her way up and down the rows. She did not want to miss a single dog because she felt a huge responsibility to give each dog a chance.

Caroline stared at the first dog for a long time and she thought to herself that he may be the one. He was a scruffy-looking dog with a rough cream-colored coat. She measured every dog she saw against him, as she made her way up and down three rows. With two rows to go and still thinking that the first scruffy dog was her match, Caroline came upon the next to the last row.

A black and white terrier mix with a white tipped tale that had been dyed bright blue (as is common in Korean grooming) caught her attention. She was enamored with that little dog. She stared at him and thought, He's the one.

Caroline was ready to take him out for a walk until she heard a faint whimper. She looked at the cage next to the blue terrier. The cage was on the bottom of a stack that was three cages tall. There was a small dog with huge eyes and odd-looking ears that were sticking out to the side. He was standing up pressing his front legs against the top of the crate to try to get Caroline's attention. As she acknowledged him, Oliver Drew's (Oli for short) ears flattened against his head and he let out another soft whimper. He was the one.

Caroline immediately asked the shelter volunteer if she could use a leash and collar to take Oli on a walk to get to know him more. The ID card on his crate indicated he had been picked up from the streets in September. It was now the first week of December and he had not yet had a walk. She carefully opened the crate door and Oli was nervous to come out. Caroline sat on the floor and talked to him until he was comfortable. He came forward and Caroline was able to get the collar on him and take him outside.

As she walked him away from the shelter, he started to prance and explore, but he was very cautious and apprehensive about his surroundings. A car drove by and in his nervousness, he flattened to the ground. Caroline reassured him and they continued the walk. She noticed an elderly woman walking in their direction. Oli did not seem concerned about the stranger approaching, so they continued. As they approached and were about to cross paths, the elderly woman stuck her hand in her purse to look for something, rustling some plastic.

The pup stopped, directed his full attention to her and wagged his tail as if he were waiting for a tasty snack. This broke Caroline's heart because it was clear that at some point in his previous life he had learned about tasty snacks.

After about a twenty-minute walk, Caroline was certain Oli was the next member of their family. When they got back to the shelter, she was heartbroken to find out that the adoption policy stated that she had to wait until the following weekend to pick him up. She didn't sleep for a week, worrying about him every day. Caroline hated to think about him in that tiny wire cage in a cold and noisy room.

The day they were able to return to get him, Caroline and a friend went together because Megan could not get off work. At the shelter, the eager Caroline immediately went to Oli to free him from his crate, but he was again uncertain. She felt so sad that he wasn't sure about leaving his crate, but decided to be patient and let him come to her when he was ready. Eventually, he came out and they made their way into a small office to sign the paperwork.

It was wintertime and they were in full winter gear. Caroline and her friend took off their gloves, hats and scarves and put them on a chair. The friend's hat had fluffy pompom ties on each side. As Caroline was signing the paperwork, Oli found the pom-poms and very gently took them from the chair and began making his way under a table with the entire hat. Caroline took the hat away and told Oli he could have as many toys as he wanted, but that they needed to get home first. She likes to think that he understood her.

Caroline carried on with signing the papers when suddenly Oli started having a meltdown. He started throwing himself against the door to get back to the crate-filled room. He started screaming and howling. It was such a strong level of desperation and it had them baffled.

Caroline carried on with signing the papers when suddenly Oli started having a meltdown. He started throwing himself against the door to get back to the crate-filled room. He started screaming and howling. It was such a strong level of desperation and it had them baffled. That's when Caroline heard the sounds of food bowls being filled. Oli was missing his dinner. To soothe him, the volunteer was kind enough to get him a few bites to eat in the office before they left, and that seemed to make him feel better.

Remember how they got there? Yes, by public transportation for an hour and a half. South Korean public transportation rules required all dogs to be in carry bags. So Caroline put Oli in the bag she brought for him, and he panicked. He panicked for the whole twenty-minute taxi ride to the train station, which meant she had to seriously overtip the driver. By this time, Oli was screaming and clawing at the bag's opening to the point that Caroline was worried he would break free. In her desperation to get home and free him from his stress, Caroline accidentally got on the wrong train. This mistake caused her to stand between train cars with her panicked pooch for a two-hour train ride and then take a forty-minute taxi ride home.

By the time they got home, Oli had made himself sick and was covered in filth. Caroline took him to the shower and tried to clean him. Oli hated the bath, but he let her do it. As a reward, Oli was given his first toy! It was a soft toy shaped like a croissant. He was so happy to get his very own toy that he snatched it out of her hand and ran around the studio flat until he found an appropriate place to bury it (in the folded-up throw blanket that was across the end of the bed.) To this day, many toys have come and gone, but he still has that croissant toy.

THEN AND NOW

Oli lives with his moms and his little sister, Lily, in Portland, Oregon. He loves treats, walks, and adventuring with his family! Oli is working toward his goal of becoming a professional tree-climber, because, well… squirrels!

AS WRITTEN BY CAROLINE

We have been through an amazing journey together. Oli came to us fearful, but determined to be an adventurer. He was scared of a boiling kettle. He was scared of the sounds of a light switch being turned on. Riding in taxis, subways, and trains was terrifying. The sounds of busy Korean streets made him cower. Walking in and out of our building meant we had to ask the security guards that Oli was fearful of offering him treats. It wasn't long before Oli was friends with all of the security guards, and he would wander to the security station after his walks to wait for his treat and acknowledgement of his adorableness. And this was only a short time before his first international move to America. In seven years, he has lived in America, South Africa, and Korea. He is our adventurous, people-loving, world-traveling foodie, and we can't imagine life without him.

Otter (Abby's brother)

Breed: Pug

Found or Adopted: December 2015 from the Seattle Pug Rescue

Amanda and Steve had a rescue pug named B.B. (Baby Bear). who had sadly passed away. B.B. was a tie-out dog, meaning she was tied to a dog house all day, so her behavior reflected only at a puppy's level. After almost a year of bonding together, the couple wanted a companion and sister for B.B. They went to Seattle Pug Rescue to find another young female pug that needed a good home.

The couple was visiting a foster home to meet a female pug when they met Otter. He was another foster in the home. They were told he was a bit standoffish, and due to his shy nature, the previous visitors had not been interested in him. Ironically, Otter was very interested in them and followed Amanda, Steve, and B.B. Fortunately, B.B. was also interested in Otter and he was in her! That night, Otter was constantly on Amanda's mind. The next day, Amanda called the foster mom and told her that Otter was the one. The foster mom offered to drop Otter off at their house that night along with the adoption papers.

It was a rainy late evening in December when he arrived. Otter briefly greeted his new parents and then ran around the living room constantly sniffing. Amanda and Steve took him for a walk and invited him to sleep in their bed that night. He settled right in on Amanda's pillow like he had known her already. The couple knew he might mark around their home, howl when they were gone, and not know the rules of the house at first. A new house is always an adjustment and they were prepared. But to their surprise, Otter was a perfect gentleman.

The couple did not know what to expect at first. The rescue had no information on him except that he was a stray found in Kirkland, Washington, and had been taken to the local animal control to find his owner. Nobody ever claimed him and that was how he ended

up in a rescue. They were also unsure of his age and family history, but they knew they were excited to make a future with him and their pug girl, B.B.

THEN AND NOW

Otter now lives in Puyallup, Washington, with Abby. B.B. and Otter bonded instantly and are inseparable. They became so close in such a short amount of time that it was more than what the couple could have ever dreamed for. Amanda was also developing a relationship with Otter and starting to cuddle with him during this time. Unfortunately, B.B. passed away suddenly from a seizure disorder, and while they grieved for a long time, Otter and Amanda became even closer in the process.

AS WRITTEN BY AMANDA

He has a funny routine of licking his neck before bedtime as if to relax me. And he also nurses the crook of my arm sometimes as if to relax himself. He also knows when I have a migraine and will lay quietly next to me. Otter actually has let out a low growl to not let anyone near me that would be disturbing me while I was resting.

While he is a very docile and sweet pug, he definitely has an inert sense to protect me. He knows when it's a day that I'm sad as he lays his head on me. I can tell he gets sad when I must go to work. He lights up when I return and often howls. He likes to be everywhere I am and will kiss me only. Or he asks to sit in my lap, so I know he feels like he has found his forever person. These days when we get into bed at night he often gets comfy and then lovingly stares at me for several minutes. It fills my heart to know that I am his everything!

Otter has his own Facebook page www.facebook.com/otter.popz (Aka 'Otter pop Pug')

Smudge

Breed: Anatolian shepherd, white Swiss shepherd,
German shepherd, German shorthaired pointer, and other mix

Found or Adopted: July 2017 from Loved at Last Dog Rescue in British Columbia, a rescue that focuses on rescuing dogs from overseas who have been tortured and abused

Marna and her husband, Craig, decided to adopt a dog, because, well... "a house is not a home without a dog." They were made aware of the plight of the dogs from Iran through their daughter (Gypsy's mom) who had adopted their dog through the same rescue group, Loved at Last Dog Rescue. They had read through all of the dogs' stories online. When they read the story about Smudge, their hearts melted and they knew he was the one.

Smudge was found as a young puppy on the streets of Tehran, Iran, emaciated and covered in wounds and blind in one eye. It was not clear if the wounds were from people torturing him, which is not uncommon in Iran, or because he was not able to defend himself against other street dogs. His blindness was most likely from the canine distemper disease, a contagious and serious disease caused by a virus that attacks the respiratory, gastrointestinal, and nervous systems of puppies and dogs. Smudge was fortunate that a loving person had found him.

This loving person wanted to care for the dog, but Smudge was very, very sick with distemper, causing him fever, coughing, and catarrh. This person was able to give him care through another angel, a loving veterinarian. They named him "Miracle" as they did not think he would live. But after being at the veterinarian for over two months, Smudge recovered.

Smudge was then cared for by a woman who worked with the rescue group until he found his forever home. The soon-to-be dog parents traveled to the Vancouver International Airport in Vancouver, B.C.,to bring Smudge home with them. Marna and Craig were anxiously and

waiting when they saw someone come out of baggage claim with a dog crate. They leapt to their feet. There he was!

Marna had to fight back tears. She was so happy. Smudge was so thin and confused and missing hair from under his left eye. He was unhealthy, hungry, thirsty, and frail, but had one sweet and loving eye looking back at them.

The ride home was a long three hours, but Smudge was calm and quiet, and their hearts were all full and at peace.

THEN AND NOW

Smudge now lives in Port Orchard, Washington. He also has a part-time foster brother, Roland, and Alexi (when Gypsy and Alexi come to visit). He loves to go for walks in the woods near his home and he brings so much joy to everyone he meets.

AS WRITTEN BY MARNA

The trust Smudge has shown after being through horrible experiences is truly amazing. He has adapted well to our family and our cat. He just wants to play with all creatures. He had kennel cough, a highly contagious respiratory disease, right after we brought him home. He unfortunately had terrible teeth as a result of the distemper virus. We had no choice but to have whatever teeth he had left extracted. We are happy to share that he is doing well. He has gained 39 pounds since we brought him home, over doubling his weight, and is now at a healthy 65 pounds! He is our love and joy.

Taj

Breed: Wolfhound and Bull Arab mix

Found or Adopted: June 2015 from Grafton, NSW, Australia

Kara knew a lady named Liza who rescued, rehabilitated, and rehomed animals before they got sent to the pound. One night, Liza came to Kara's house with the sweetest little puppy dog for her and her family to meet. This puppy was adorable with massive feet, cuddly, tan, tiny, and soft. In less than five minutes of being together, the family knew that the pup would join them. What they learnt next about their boy, Taj, was so saddening.

Liza had rescued Taj just over a week earlier after seeing an advertisement on Facebook about someone giving away a sick puppy. The people who put up the ad told her that if she didn't pick him up immediately, they would "find other means of getting rid of him." Liza had arrived to a lifeless, sad puppy.

Now, Taj is healthy and happy and it's scary to think his life could have been cut so short. He is a crazy, lanky, goofball. Life would be much duller without him around. He's a giant lap dog that doesn't completely understand his size.

THEN AND NOW

Taj and Kara now live in South Grafton, NSW, Australia. After bonding with most of the family, Taj slept with Kara every night as a puppy. Kara takes him to the beach at least once a week and walks him every other day so they spend quite a lot of time together. Although he was only with his rescuer for a week, every time they see Liza on our walks, Taj runs right up to her and jumps all over her. It seems as if he is thanking her for giving him a second chance at life.

AS WRITTEN BY KARA

Since last time we spoke our love for this goofball has grown more than we could imagine! He makes us laugh (except for when he pees on children's sand castles) and keeps us safe. Taj has grown a love for water and would follow us out the back of the surf if he didn't get barreled by waves. His birthday is March 18th and is growing older, but shows absolutely no signs of slowing down. He's still running rings around everyone and everything and takes me on walks!

Theodore (Theo)

Breed: Border collie mix

Found or Adopted: July 2017 from a dog rescue in Canada

Alexa grew up with dogs but wanted a dog of her own. When she finally bought her first house, it did not feel like home. She needed a dog. Alexa wanted to adopt because there were so many dogs that needed a home. She searched for months and months, checking out lots of rescues and the Society for the Prevention of Cruelty to Animals (SPCA). She met a few dogs, but nothing really clicked. Alexa wanted it to be a good fit for both her and the dog.

Then Theo came along. He was one of three siblings of the Chipmunk litter: Alvin, Simon, and Theodore. Their background is unknown and they had come to the rescue as fluffy little pups. Alvin and Simon got adopted fairly quickly. Theo did too, but ended up being returned to the rescue as the family did not know what they were getting into with this little ball of energy.

The foster family worked really hard, and Theo was adopted again. Unexpected circumstances came up for the second owner, and Theo found himself returned to the rescue yet again. The rescue and fosters never gave up on little Theo. Then in the summer of 2017, Alexa came upon his bio and she had to meet him.

Theo and Alexa met at a local off-leash dog park, and Alexa felt the click. She knew right away that this spunky little guy was the dog for her! Within a week or so, everything was finalized and Theo moved into his forever home. Third time's the charm, they say!

Theo and Alexa found their way to each other just over a week before Alexa's grandfather's passing.

Alexa and her grandfather were very close, and it was incredibly difficult for her to say goodbye. Alexa hadn't realized it earlier that Theodore was the name of her grandfather's hometown. It was meant to be. Theo kept Alexa to a routine through this difficult time of losing a loved one. Theo got Alexa out of bed when she otherwise would have been staying inside, struggling and sad. Alexa had come to need Theo just as much as he needed her.

THEN AND NOW

Now Theo lives on the prairies of Saskatchewan, Canada. Due to Theo's unsettled and unfair start to life, Alexa and Theo had to work on a lot of things to overcome his many insecurities and fears. From Theo cowering and hiding when Alexa walked past his crate to voluntarily going into the crate when Alexa got ready for work, a lot of progress was made. Theo has since overcome his separation anxiety, and no longer takes apart any door jams or couches. In the beginning, they did an obedience class together, and Alexa realized that Theo was one smart cookie because he learned very quickly. Theo has completed agility and rally obedience classes, and he is a rockstar! He especially loves the tunnel and jumps. They work on trust every day, and he loves to play with his friends and sticks, and appreciates a good nap under a sunbeam on Sunday mornings.

AS WRITTEN BY ALEXA

Some dogs just really need to be given a chance to blossom into the awesome dogs they really are! There are no perfect dogs, no perfect people; just perfect fits!

Turks

Breed: Pitbull mix

Found or Adopted: September 2017 from the island St. Croix in the Virgin Islands in the Caribbean, after which he was brought to Nate's Honor Animal Rescue in Bradenton, Florida

In December 2016, Alycia and Joe lost their beloved Kobe, a German shepherd/Lab mix. He was their first pet together and was very dear to them. Along with two other small dogs, the family waited an entire year and finally felt that the time was right to get another dog. They decided to go to Nate's Honor Animal Rescue to see if they connected with any of the dogs. Alycia and Joe were adamant about adopting rather than buying from a breeder. Joe wanted to go specifically look at a dog he had found on the rescue's website.

When they arrived, that particular dog was in the process of being adopted by the couple just before them. Still, they decided to go take a look at the available dogs. That's when they came upon Turks. Turks was one of four in his litter and was the only boy. The litter had been rescued from St. Croix after Hurricane Irma had hit. Turks was only a month old when they found him. He was nine pounds, emaciated, and scavenging for food. You could see his ribs, and he had patches of fur missing all over. Due to the lack of nutrition, the bone structure of Turk's front legs was not strong enough to stand straight, resulting in his entire paw being turned outward, and his legs becoming bowlegged to support the way he had to walk.

After two weeks of quarantine, with no human contact, Turks was transferred to the University of Florida where he went through intensive testing. From disease and contamination tests to X-rays on the bone structure, it was determined there was no other damage other than lack of nutrition. Turks' three sisters were all adopted immediately, but after countless visits with many, many families who came to look at Turks, every family decided against him once they heard of his paw difficulty, until Alycia and Joe!

When the rescue let Alycia and Joe know how many families had passed on Turks, they looked at each other and immediately knew he was the one. In Alycia's heart, she knew that the point of rescuing a dog was also accepting them with all of their imperfections and giving them a life they could never have dreamed of. Turks was a dog who truly deserved a rescue after what he had gone through, and they were determined to give that to him. It just so happened that the Virgin Islands were also very dear to the couple. That was where the couple had gotten engaged and a dear family friend owned a house in St. Thomas, so they visited quite often. It was like the stars aligned and Turks was absolutely meant for their family.

THEN AND NOW

Turks lives with his mom and dad in Parrish, Florida. He loves spending time with his little big brothers, Jacob and Griffin (a five-pound Chorkie and seven-pound Chihuahua, respectively), doing laps around the backyard, practicing for a career in competitive racing, and catching a snooze under the covers. Initially, Turks was very well-behaved—Alycia and Joe joke that this was his honeymoon phase of winning them over. Like any true puppy, Turks went through the chewing stage, which included everything from an iPhone, remote controls, TV consoles, and lots of pillow cushions. Their love for him didn't waver, though. Even after the condition that he was in initially, he still had all the love in the world to give and perfected the master of puppy eyes! Turks is a healthy fifty-five pounds and still as much of a cuddler as he was in the beginning. There's nothing he loves more than wrapping his body around Alycia and his face in her neck. He's a lovebug.

AS WRITTEN BY ALYCIA

Since adopting Turks, he has proven to be the best puppy we could have ever asked for. He has not once had an accident in the house, never cried when we put him in the cage at night (though after four days he was already in the bed with us), and has done no damage to our house or belongings. He is the most loving, energetic puppy full of life, and I already can't imagine our lives without him. After only two weeks, his paw had already drastically improved itself and we are still working daily on helping him get stronger and grow to be a normal healthy puppy. No matter what, we will always love him for all of his imperfections because to us he is perfect.

Turks was very reserved when we first took him home (and for good reason)! He had a rough life before us and we knew it would take time for him to warm up to us until he could trust us. The first few days he was shy and would stay in several "comfort" spots around the house, slowly exploring new areas of the house when he was ready. He has so much love to give and it showed immediately. He loves being as close to us as possible and literally sleeps on top of us every chance he gets. If I sit down on the ground, he is immediately in my lap and he loves to be picked up and held like a baby. He now travels through every part of the house, attempts to jump on the couch (with no success, so we have to help him every time), and loves trying to get our other two dogs to play with him. There are toys scattered in every inch of the house, and a few in our bed when he gets bored and wants to play while everyone else is sleeping, but I wouldn't change a thing!

T'va

Breed: Unknown breed - possibly a terrier mix

Found or Adopted: December 14, 2014, from Mulege, B.C.S., Mexico

On December 14, 2014, a tiny little town of Mulege, B.C.S., Mexico, with one gas pump and one bank, and also a world-class diving destination by the Sea of Cortez, had a peculiar happening. Annabelle and her boyfriend were on their drive back home to California when Anabelle stopped by the ATM in the center of the town. Suddenly, she spotted a tiny little dog scurrying across the street, almost getting hit by a car at the four-way stop.

Annabelle had to make sure the puppy was okay. She ran from the car and scooped up the scared pup, T'va. The puppy cowered in fear and covered herself. Annabelle wrapped T'va in a towel and took her back to the car when she noticed that the puppy was covered in engorged ticks from her face to her bum.

They drove to the nearest rest stop to bathe her in the bathroom sink and pull off all her ticks with tweezers. Annabelle lost count after forty ticks. The water turned red as she bathed her. After every tick was taken off, clean T'va was taken back to the car to be fed. First, Annabelle gave T'va milk. The pup drank it all up like she hadn't drank anything in days. Then, T'va snatched the bread from Annabelle's purse and scarfed it down. She even devoured a second slice. After her feast, T'va, wrapped in a towel, fell asleep, safe and full.

As Annabelle looked at the dog asleep in her lap, she felt her heart fill with a love she had never felt before. Annabelle couldn't imagine leaving T'va anywhere or with anyone else because she wanted to make sure she was happy and healthy. From that moment on, T'va was Annabelle's.

Halfway through their journey, Annabelle thought that T'va might need a bathroom break. The second T'va was let down from the car, she bolted for cover, and the poor thing found it in a spiny cactus and yelped in pain.

Annabelle's boyfriend reached in and grabbed T'va out, sustaining several cactus spines to his hand and all over the puppy's body. They carefully pulled them off before traveling another thirteen hours to the U.S. border.

Upon arrival, the agent asked two questions: "What were you doing in Mexico?" and "Where are you headed?" Both the questions were answered, but they never mentioned T'va, who was asleep in the back. The agent waved them through, and they booked it for the nearest vet. After examining her teeth and weight of only 3 lb, the vet determined that T'va was about three months old and in perfect health. They were free to call T'va theirs forever!

THEN AND NOW

T'va now lives with her mom and dad in Edmonds, Washington. She loves to look out the window for any possible signs of movement, and will alert you if anything is out of sorts. T'va loves exploring the Pacific Northwest, and especially loves romping in the snow and going on long, secluded hikes. She is a road trip warrior and frequent flier on Alaska Airlines. She is the best travel companion anybody could ever hope for!

AS WRITTEN BY ANNABELLE

Initially, T'va was scared and did not trust us immediately. Today, she is still that way with strangers, but once she trusts you, you have a friend for life. T'va and I have a truly unique bond. We've done puppy obedience all the way through preparation for the canine good citizen test. We've also done all levels of agility together. This kind of work requires a strong and special bond between dog and parent. We do everything together, from errands to road trips, even to traveling across the country! We just love being and doing everything together, and I can't imagine my life without her.